GALAXY IN THRALL

This is a limited edition of 100 copies

and this is number: */ 100*

Copyright ©2019 by James Bertolino

All rights reserved.

Published by Goldfish Press

4545 42nd Avenue Southwest

Suite 211

Seattle, Washington, 98116

Manufactured in the United States of America

ISBN 13: 978-1-950276-05-9

ISBN 10: 1-950276-05-8

Library of Congress Catalog Card Number 2019915372

Cover design by: J. Edward Moss

Book design by: Susan Steiner

This book was set on the Monotype Bookman Old

GALAXY IN THRALL

Poems by
James Bertolino

Goldfish Press

TABLE OF CONTENTS

Ocean Breakfast	2
Bums Rush	3
At the Bookfair	4
The Bone Dowser	5
Soft Belly, Open Heart	6
Gaia Spins	7
Liquid Recall	8
Cattails	9
User Friendly	10
Black Root	11
Bird Karma	12
Changeling	13
Astral Projection	14
Chicken Plucker	15
A Blind Man	16
Choice	17
The Boulder	18
Change of Life	19
Advance	20
The Bowl	21
The Muffin	22
Composing Love: A Blues Sonnet	23
You Are My Ocean	24
Bird	25
Prayer	26
The Dream	27
Dying Doesn't Run	28
The Crab Doesn't Fear	29
Chewing	30

The Dreamer	31
No Underlings	32
Consider the Owl	34
The Confection	35
The Guniverse	36
Galaxy in Thrall	37
Coy Science	38
Schadenfreud	39
The Brink	40

Ocean Breakfast

Fog leans over
the Sound.

The gulls and crows
jabber at the blue teeth
of our cook-stove.

Today it will be pancakes
enhanced with buttermilk
and currants.

The Bums Rush

The bums rush toward
that blue
season
the creamy
half-day morning glories own
before their spirals
collapse

for hours so intimate with the sky,
now small wrinkled sobs
of purple:

embarrassments
along the sinewy vine.

At The Bookfair

Near the center, creating
an island of turbulence

in the bookish herd, and sounding
like two elephant cows

crooning to the little ones,
were huddled the wheelchair

poets, palsied of body
and speech, but of love

strong, of love clear.

The Bone Dowser

A leap of yodel
charisma
means more
to the family than
Aunt Gertie's gram
of companionship.

We don't need drugs
to remember the day she married
the bone dowser—it affected
our plans. Dad lost his business
and Mom took to scrawling "hornet
paper"
on church envelopes. She licked
the flaps and stuck them
to everything, including my tub raft,
the woozy dutch elm, and
the Mayor's fish tank.

Thankfully only Dad did time.

Thankfully several hours
have passed. Never mind the wheel
chair, the floatation devices,
it's the buzzing in my marrow
that has me slipping. Next week
Uncle Georgie intends to begin
dowsing dogs.

Soft Belly, Open Heart

"We think the fire eats the wood. We are wrong.
The wood reaches out to the flame." —Jack Gilbert

Soft belly, open heart, let what flows
flow uninhibited. Let the helical curve

of the ear be kissed, the structure of bones
be lightly stroked. Open now to the intelligence

carried by a taste, or in light shaping a divan.
You can know what holds you beyond this bright

falling of matter, and you may be penetrated.
The cells are ready—they will blink more messages

than you can comprehend. And when life comes
to what bleeds, what burns, don't wait

for the fire. It is waiting for you.

Gaia Spins

Just say "moss" and see
where it takes you:

to those tiny atmospheric
organs that wave above

the green pillowing
of a small planet: Sufi spinning

her galactic dream. She runs
her tongue over her lips,

and a thunderstorm drenches
the Mojave Desert. When she makes

a fist, spontaneous combustion
illuminates a mountain cave.

Now white formations
on the underside of an eagle's

wing are the syllables
of change. Forever beach crabs

will carry her portrait, and clam
siphons rise to whistle her name.

Liquid Recall

Burbling below where I've settled
on a mossy boulder,
the creek is running
with the millions of memories

this water has carried since it was snow
in the Himalayas,
where Yeti shit
may have darkened it.

Memories of the cougar's urine,
rich with excess protein.
Memories of the vapor
when Jesus exhaled one chill night

in the desert.

Cattails

The stalks of cattails
rise out of the pond
like prayers whispered
by the faithful—so slim
and green, so grateful for both
water and sunlight.

And just beyond, the glorious
cloud of tiny yellow-green leaves
on the willow rising from the island
wishing them well.

User Friendly

Quietly repeating
its known sound,

the last of the genetically
unmodified species

descend into the planet's first
true silence.

At the funeral, concerned
cybercitizens exchange

scratch and sniff
remorse cards.

Black Root

An elbow
of black root

breaks through
a cushion

of green moss.
In the near

distance
the chick, chick,

chuckle of water
as it scallops

the shore.

Bird Karma

We develop unsightly knobs
on our beaks,
and before we're done with
self-consciousness

we're thrashing at our shells

Wringing our stringy
featherless necks
to be free.

Changeling

Imagine an entity that resembles
a flock of a million tiny birds.

This living creature changes shape,
speed, and direction with the
randomness

of play, of pleasure. It exists
in outer space, its life not limited

by feeding, responsibility,
or age. Its purpose, simply,

is to change.

Astral Projection

Body stripped
away like
insulation from
a high-voltage
line.

Chicken Plucker

Being a chicken plucker could have been
a good job. Folks have always loved chicken,
and the pluckers were key.

Sure, small farmers
did their own plucking, but the families that nation-
wide bought millions of chickens
each year could only put them in their pots
and on their grills if the many hundreds of pluckers
kept their jobs.

Nowadays the chicken-production
companies probably employ some clever, automated
systems for denuding the birds of feathers.
Running a chicken-plucking machine isn't the same
as proudly wearing the title Chicken Plucker.

A Blind Man

I am blind,
fondling
legless spiders
and the ant-spattered hammer,
mouth dripping with the custard
of a toad's brain.

The smell of pee on hot coals
tickles my nose.
I wish I could eat glass.

If my god would make me
a mattress of pubic fur,
and present an earthen jug
filled with the cool
of seaweed
and fresh mushrooms

to soothe my hot eyes

I would lie quietly,
and accept all this.

Choice

When we make a turning
half-step in our lives
and are taken by an ecstasy

that addles the water
in our cells, that cloaks
the deepest organs in a glow,

we do not lean coolly away
and consider from whence
this enlivening has come.

We are in every strand
grateful for this moment
that proves the soul.

We must accept this fondling
of the gods, or ever be
orphans of choice.

The Boulder

When will this be over,
asks the boulder. So long

since I've smelled
a blossom, or been tickled.

Never have I complained
of snow or wind or fire.

How will I know
when my work is done?

Change of Life

When the sparrow
kicked me

in the shins, it left
an ugly bruise.

Now I'm embarrassed
to wear my cut-offs in public.

Who would have thought
that feathery flier

could be dangerous?
You might feel

threatened by the anaconda,
but an earthworm?

Imagine having found
a life-changing haiku.

Advance

I speak with an uncivil
tongue, and

invite you to advance
for a bruising. Be the planet.

Be the advent of the holoreal,
where nothing

achieves itself without
achieving all.

The Bowl

Side-by-side,
sliced bananas
and pears.

There is enough
liquor to float islands
of fruit, enough

desire. The bowl,
with its perfect circle,
denies division.

We need not want
what we are
the middle of.

The Muffin

There might soon
come the day
for a multi-berry
bran muffin—
speaking metaphorically
of course.
It will certainly be
a wholesome new
experience: a pastry hug.
I may feel like I finally belong—
this world would have a place for me.
I remember now, with some dismay,
how when my younger brother
and I misbehaved, my father
would kick our butts
with his pointy dress shoes
to demonstrate his displeasure.
That was at least sixty years
ago, and now I experience
this world
kicking my ass.

Composing Love: A Blues Sonnet

If only I could compose at will
the poem that, beyond failure,
will open my lover's heart

and fill her chambers with what makes
her feelings for me more smooth
than anything that charmed her youth.

Then I know our love would be right,
and she would hold to a man who writes
the kind of lines that brighten

her days with spirit that touches.
She knows shaped life requires touch,
while death devises clouds that stretch

all into shadowed distance. Our hands
together could fashion poems of celestial
weather.

You Are My Ocean

The ocean is immense,
beyond measure, while my heart
is small, flooded with
its drop of weakness.

I will go with the ocean,
will accept that great,
and constant,
love.

Bird

Mystery rises.
Warm sap enters each nerve-twig

and branch, loads the tree
of her body. Suddenly

she has an aura of leaves.
Now a wind sets her shimmering

in the moonlight and
a great bird descends.

Prayer

The two of them agreed to discuss
suicide
over brunch. Now she finds herself
repelled by the cologne on this man
who claims he was once a feral cat.

He says he respects her because
she was a trainer of dogs.
So she presses on by saying her attitude
about the world can be summed-up
in a single sentence: "The worst name
I've been called is true."

She tells him that on her way to meet
him, she stooped
to pick up a single bloody feather, and
she has
questions that need answers: Why are
bag-ladies
wearing ski-masks; why do the torturers
argue
over subtle religious differences; and
why
last night did a sweet peace marcher
hold a blade at her throat.

"I have only a single answer to your
troubles,"
he replied: "After I leave you,
pray for amnesia."

The Dream

When you respond
to events around you
as though they were real

and have consequences,
then you commit yourself
to the authority of the dream.

But if you recognize what happens
is not real, you know yourself
to be the dreamer. You see the world

as the story you are telling, a play
where the parts have incarnated
from a place where all hands

touch all hearts.

Dying Doesn't Run

You say, "Dying
doesn't run
in my family."

To live beyond mortality,
you must die, daily, and
with no complaint.

To have everything,
you accept anything
because the actual

can never be contained.
Because syllables gather
to comprise a new being.

Whatever gains presence
has always been anticipated,
will ever remain.

The Crab Doesn't Fear

When you see the crab
moving sideways

in the shadows, you should know
its glossy shell not only protects,

but imprisons. When finally it wrenches
its swelling flesh free, it is flayed

by pain, naked to every least abrasion,
each bite. But the crab doesn't fear

its life is finished. It soon feels itself
loose
and lengthened, skin hardening

to new armor. Finds itself grown
more grand, commanding and

fiercely hungry.

Chewing

Awakened long after midnight
to the sound of someone chewing
in the dark, she listened so intently

her jaw muscles ached. At first just
beyond
the edge of recognition, but then she
knew
the truth: it was a warning

from adolescence that had arrived
too late. There was a man who'd always
spoken with his mouth full. He used

football analogies when he described
his sex life, when he explained
how he would hurt her.

"It's like, you've got to control the ball.
What gets in your way goes down.
And remember, even

a kitten has claws—
but I'm a Tom!"

The Dreamer

He knew she was a Dreamer,
that during love her limbs
would map the universe.

He needed to find her before
the Cavern Men run their ruinous
plan, their autumnal theology.

Together they might prevent
the fall from sentience.

When at last he held her,
they rocked through each other
under the oaks of ritual.

A curled leaf rattled
as a slug moved it rich muscle past.
Greenish yellow and spotted black—the
planet
steadied for that contact.

She said, "My Love, now recognize
your long-eyed sister
in the damp grass."

No Underlings

I am wearing my chthonic underwear,
but it's not an issue. One might
consider
that above ground, or in the
underworld,
we all need underwear. Sure, I could go
naked,

as I have to board meetings, but it's not
a policy
with me. I appreciate the elastic
suspension,
the apprehension a stranger might
experience
that suggests super-, or even non-
human

attributes contained by certain
garments.
All I ask is an opportunity to express
what
I've risen to give, emerged to provide.
Those who have invited me into their
domiciles

have felt rewarded. More than certainty,
it's hope
I am after, and the comfort I might
present.
Sure, I've heard the naysayers who say
"shitonic," but they lose, they lisp like
weak

fish. Come join the Thonic Brotherhood,
sisters welcome. Don't dwell
on what smacks of blisters and blood.
As Orwell meant to say, let's get down!

Consider the Owl

When you consider the owl,
face shaped like a heart,
you might tend to visualize
someone you've loved, perhaps
a girl, or a woman, who has left
this world. What else is gone?

Could it be the innovative brain
you depended on? The muscles
that thickened your arms, shoulders
and chest? And what about
your determination to be of value
to the world?

When the owl feels sleepy,
does he take a nap?

The Confection

I've seen her control
strange men
with her eyelids.

A warm hallucination brushes
her cheek, and turning,
she sees a light blue limb
wrinkle the atmosphere.

Learning to love her body
more gently, she tells me: "These
little deaths taste like butter
and brine."

As violins begin to play,
millions of chocolate chips
become part of our
embrace.

The Guniverse

Welcome to the Guniverse,
where we practice Dog Yoga.
Never without a nurse,
we shoot and shout *oogah!*

Gar Head is our teacher.
Wombat the boss.
Don't even come near
if you talk with a lisp.

The weak play philosophy,
while the virile sing.
We welcome bruised knees
and mind-chains that ring.

Are you an addict?
Twisted by confusion?
Here you can connect
with a soul transfusion.

Sure we'll take your bucks
and make you wash the floor,
but you'll be awestruck
when you're kicked out the door.

Galaxy in Thrall

I speak with an uncivil tongue.
No effort, no cause for alarm.

Blister or scrape, the beauty
of skin stretched thin.

I invite her to advance
for a bruising. Be the planet.

Be the advent of the holoreal,
where nothing achieves itself

without achieving all.
Her tender kiss, my galaxy.

My eyes, her eyes, ours.
We see ourselves, where time

is an opinion. Her space
interpenetrates, while mine

is endless repetition.
Together we hold the world.

Coy Science

Need we be responsible
for the aural creatures created
when a guitar chord is strummed?
The survival of such transitory
populations would surely
reward support.

And when it comes to the conceptual shape
generated by an odor, how can we fail
to identify it as fully proprietary?

Most troubling, perhaps, is the unique
molecular structures engineered
by the increasing density of our waste.
What we discard holds a special position,
and it's high time the Nobel Prize committee
recognize the value of unintentional genius.

Schadenfreud

There are certain
public figures
with grand responsibilities
who thrill me when
they fail.

Don't get me wrong,
I do wish that our civilization
would thrive, yet feel philosophically
embarrassed when
my own inspired efforts
succeed.

One of the great thinkers
of our modern world—Sigmund
Freud—is reputed to have said:
"Religion is an illusion."

And thinking again of those public
figures, Freud also insisted that,
"Yes, America is gigantic,
but a gigantic mistake."

The Brink

When is the rock a pillow?
How can a cracked branch
bring the sought?
If dunes move like the tides,
and clouds spread insects that fall
as bright petals, are we nearing the end?

You know a voice as yellow.
An odor is the number nine.
The body that has long carried you
becomes an avalanche bringing a new
shape.
What is grand has finished, and your
last breath
lifts its wings over the brink.

===

James Bertolino's poetry has received recognition through a Book-of-the-Month Club Poetry Fellowship, the Discovery Award, a National Endowment for the Arts fellowship, two *Quarterly Review of Literature* book publication awards, and the Jeanne Lohmann Poetry Prize for Washington State Poets. He has had numerous chapbooks and 12 volumes of poetry published, the most recent being *Ravenous Bliss: New and Selected Love Poems*, 2014, from MoonPath Press. In 2017 he edited an anthology of poems which, in various ways, refer to alcohol -- including work by American poets from 31 states and four countries. The volume was published in 2018 by World Enough Writers Press in Tillamook, Oregon. Since 1965, he has had his own poetry reprinted in 48 anthologies, and in 1968 he edited the *Northwest Poets* anthology published by Quixote Press. His own publishing efforts included *Abraxas* magazine and Press, as well as Stone-Marrow Press. He received his Bachelor's degree from the University of Wisconsin-Oshkosh, and his MFA from Cornell University, where he served as assistant editor for Ithaca House Books and poetry editor for

Cornell's *Epoch* magazine. He taught creative writing for 36 years at Cornell, University of Cincinnati, Western Washington University and, in 2006, retired from a position as Writer-in-Residence at Willamette University in Oregon. He and his partner, poet and artist Anita Boyle, live on five acres near Bellingham, Washington. In 2012 Bertolino served as judge for the California Federation of Chaparral Poets competition, and 2019 was the tenth year that, as a board member of the Before Columbus Foundation in Berkeley, he chose a book for an American Book Award.

www.ingramcontent.com/pod-product-compliance
Lightning Source LLC
LaVergne TN
LVHW011431080426
835512LV00005B/380